KICK THE OLD MAN OUT

CHAPTER ONE

Introduction

A lot of people want to write a novel. I never had that desire which is convenient because this is not a novel. I HAVE wanted to write something about living life to its fullest. I'm fortunate enough to have lived what I consider a great life. Of course it's all about perspective isn't it? I am not rich nor am I famous, but I consider myself successful nonetheless. I therefore set out to write about an average person's struggle for success and happiness. My hope is that somewhere in my musings you as the reader will recognize that you are not alone and perhaps find some tidbits of advice that will help put your own life in perspective. I use the words "find some tidbits of advice" purposefully because I can only relay what lessons I have learned that helped me overcome adversity. I cannot preach to others as to what decisions to make to achieve happiness and success, but I can at least explain how I did it. The process of making decisions is based on personal experiences and since everyone has different

1

experiences, the information used with which to decide one's course in life will necessarily yield different results. That said, perhaps somewhere in these chapters you will find commonality in your own experiences and perhaps even receive some guidance and perspective.

To be clear, I was not born into a wealthy family nor was I born into poverty. I had a roof to sleep under, a bed to sleep on, clothes to wear, and food on the table. I was the oldest of three boys. Unfortunately our youngest brother died when he was only a month old from an enlarged heart. As a result, my mother was very protective of my other brother and I. There was also a fear of calamity striking again causing our parents to teach us that we were entitled to nothing and life was more precious than "things". Thus necessities were earned, not given. We also learned that wants are much different than needs which are always taken care of first.

My parents were both raised in the country and found no reason to raise us any differently. We lived just outside of a very small town with a population of about 500 people. The county seat was 15 miles away and was considered "the city". This was situated between the big cities of Terre Haute and Indianapolis. I always considered myself as being from the country since most of the people I knew were either farmers or children of farmers. I suppose growing up in a rural area made me somewhat naïve in some ways. I wasn't exposed to crime, drug use, or politics. This shaped my belief that people were good and always wanted to do good for each other. I found later this is not always the case but my philosophy has not been swayed. I still believe in the good of man and always will. The alternative leaves a person depressed with no ambition or drive. I've seen it. Therefore I will maintain a positive outlook on life and enjoy everything life has to offer thank you very much.

The earliest memory I have is when I was about two years old. My first brother was only three months old. I remember being awakened by my mother and my aunt in the middle of the night. There were red flashing lights circling the walls of the room where I was sleeping. I could hear a lot of people and my aunt seemed to be extremely agitated for some reason. There were people

3

running in and out of the room and I could see shadows bathed in the red glowing flashes through the window. They were moving quickly back and forth and up and down. I don't remember any more from that night but mom told me the story when I was older. There had been an accident and a motorcyclist was severely injured with his leg torn open. My father made a quick tourniquet with his belt to stop his bleeding and eventually the man was taken to the hospital. I learned from my mother that on that night, my father had saved this man's life and in appreciation had given my parents some money which was used to buy a kitchen table. I'm sure there was a huge argument because every time anyone ever offered my dad money for any help or service he provided, he refused to take it. Sometimes vehemently. I'm now convinced that the only reason he accepted it was to buy that kitchen table they had for the next 50 years. He saw that table as something his family needed and certainly something that would make my mother very happy. As for my dad, he was happy knowing the man was OK and that was enough for him. I was to learn a lot from my father but it wasn't due to words or even the advice

4

he gave sparingly years later when I was almost a man. He taught by example but that didn't mean he wasn't prone to state absolutes such as, "You don't talk with your mouth full."

Dad was one of nine children raised in southern Kentucky. He was born into poverty and was not well cared for by his father. As a result he harbored resentment toward him. At about nine years old he was living with his aunt who had three daughters. Dad would call these girls his sisters for the rest of his life. It was his aunt that provided him with necessities my brothers and I took for granted such as shoes and a coat. Dad never talked much about his childhood but it was very apparent that he was a driven man determined never to live in the squalor he was born into. We went to Kentucky many times to visit our family. These trips were our vacation. We would stay with family instead of hotels. I liked staying with dad's sisters best. They had running water and indoor toilets. My grandmother and uncles had outhouses and no running water. To have water for cooking and bathing at grandma's, we had to go to the spring and fill as many jugs as we could carry. Since the spring was

5

about a half mile from the house, we at least got a lot of exercise.

Many people told stories of my grandfather always carrying a lot of cash while his children had no shoes or decent clothing. I never knew such conditions. I don't know the sacrifices dad made for my brother and me, but I know that seeing us happy and healthy was more important to him than anything imaginable. He worked for our happiness. Every life decision he made was to benefit his family. He never traveled, never wore expensive clothes, and never had expensive cars. Dad always liked cars though and as a result, I learned to like them too. Dad taught me early to know the make and model of any car driving by. Back then cars and trucks were unique. They all had different body lines and markedly different styles of trim. And every year saw new designs completely different than the year before. Nowadays major changes only happen every five to eight years. It's a lot harder to tell them apart now without seeing the badge or nameplate on the front. When I was very young dad had a 1931 Ford roadster. He was trying to restore it and over the years had purchased a lot of parts which were stored neatly under my parent's bed. I can recall him sanding the car in our small garage getting it ready for paint and the trips to the person restoring his engine. The car also became a depository for items in the garage like water hoses, laundry waiting next in line for the washer (also in the garage), and tools that needed a temporary resting place. I was about 7 years old when he sold it. He was so proud of what it was going to be and showed the buyer all the extra parts and the rumble seat that only needed upholstered. He didn't want to sell it, but that car was not a necessity for his family's support. It was his hobby which he gave up for his family. Although he never had another antique car until after my brother and I had families of our own, he continued his subscription to Hemmings Motor News every year.

As my brother and I grew, we learned about manners, respect, and proper behavior from our parents. Both of my parents were responsible for discipline and if we deserved it, we were spanked. Now I know I was spanked as a child because I can remember it. What I can't remember is any of the reasons why and I never in my life ever felt beaten or treated poorly. I do remember my mother and father telling us that they hated spanking us because they loved us and it hurt them more inside than it did us outside. But they knew if they didn't sometimes spank us that we wouldn't turn out right. (Mom loved to say it like that.) We were not hit or beaten. We were spanked. When we were very young mom and dad used their hands, then when we were older a belt was used. Mom's weapon of choice was a hot wheels track. However that all stopped when she found welts on my brother's legs after she had spanked him. Again, I don't know what the crime was, but I remember it was summer and he was wearing shorts. He was in his bed (thinking about what he had done, I'm sure) and I was playing on the floor when mom came in to check on him. She saw the welts on the back of his legs and asked what he had done. I told her it was the hot wheels track. She didn't believe it until I matched the track to his leg. I always wondered later if she left the room and cried about it but she never used a track on us again. I can't remember the last time I was spanked but I know that at least after 4th grade, I was only scolded for my crimes and misdemeanors.

One time I spoke back to my mother. Something I'm sure was disrespectful because she immediately slapped my face. Not hard but I was shocked. She immediately grabbed me and hugged me profusely apologizing and I was never slapped again. I also never disrespected my parents ever again. My brother was much more rebellious than I. He therefore received more discipline. I guess it worked well. He had a fantastic career as a state trooper followed by two terms in office as the county sheriff.

We are all shaped by our childhood. I may not have had the latest fashion to wear, expensive toys, or even traveled much, but I was loved. With that love, I learned that respect, integrity, and honesty are the only true riches. Something I strayed from later, but I eventually got back on track. It took a while for them to get it into my head, but I finally learned that the measure of a man is simply respect, integrity and honesty. Based on these tenants, I have developed my own set of rules to follow. Never make a commitment you can't keep. Never borrow anything you don't return. Never lend money you can't give freely without repayment. Always be honest. (Some

9

people think I'm too direct at times but my father used to hate it when people "beat around the bush" so I don't.) Always help others when you can without expectation of reward. Live within your means and don't worry about keeping up with the Jones's. Protect your family and keep them safe. When making life decisions, consider how it affects your family. Only when I broke any of these rules, was life hard. And I had some hard times. However, I learned from my mistakes and became a better man for it. Of course dad was right. If I had just listened to him more often, my path would have been easier. But in my defense, my stubbornness was inherited.

CHAPTER TWO

Education

So now that you know a little about my early childhood, I thought I'd separate the rest of this book into the usual topics of concern that most people have during their sojourn through life. I thought I'd start with education. This is something that dad felt was more important than anything in the world, mainly because he never had the chance to get an education. His father was a farmer and all of his children helped work on the farm so school was not a priority. Dad left his home in Kentucky when he was 14 and moved to northern Indiana. I never knew why nor how he got there, but I think it had something to do with his father's death that same year. He told me that he worked as a tree topper in Goshen, Indiana. I always thought that was so young to try to start your own life as an adult and that was in 1950. I didn't know anyone so young could go to work at that time. Anyway he eventually moved to central Indiana working in the local grain elevator company. He rented a room and I remember as a small child visiting the people he lived with during

11

those days. They liked to reminisce about the times he would "run around town" in his '57 Chevy. The story they repeated most often was about a girl that jumped in his car once while he was stopped at an intersection. Apparently he was pretty popular with the ladies. It was during that time when he met my mother at a roller skating rink. She was around 19 and he was 25. My mother said he came out on the floor while she was skating and almost knocked her over. This was because he couldn't skate. My belief is that he was only there to pick up girls. Well, maybe knock them over. At any rate his plan seemed to work with my mother.

Mom spent a lot of time at the skating rink. She had quit school at 14 to work at the local dime store to help support her family. She was the second oldest of 13 children. Roller skating was her relaxation and she was good. She danced on skates and I remember other family members and friends tell me how people would stop skating to watch her dance. I created a vision in my head of my father watching her and putting on skates to meet her. I could see him fumbling out on the floor losing his balance and at the last second grabbing my mother to prevent himself from falling. It must have been really funny to watch.

When I was 4 years old, dad got a job at the auto plant in Indianapolis and worked there the rest of his life, eventually driving a forklift in their warehouse. Dad was always a very hard worker and worked all the overtime he could. He once told me there were only two ways to get ahead in life. One was to work all the overtime you could and the other was to get a good education. He felt that he could have done a lot more for us had he only had the education his bosses had. He tied education to income and was determined that his boys would have opportunities he never had. I always felt dad was tougher on me when it came to my education than he was on my brother. He was always angry if I didn't receive all A's on my report cards, but my brother was only berated if he brought home a C. When I was in first grade, he had an incentive program for me. He would pay me for every A and a little more for an A+ but I would lose money for every B which was more than I was paid for A's. It usually worked out where I broke even at zero cash. He never accepted anything less than perfection. I remember clearly

13

when I was in fourth grade that my last report card for the year was all A's with only two B+ marks. At that time McDonald's would give a student a free ice cream cone for showing them an A on their report card. I was excited when we went there to get mine because we rarely ate out. We went inside and when I showed them my card, there was such a fuss created that the manager came out and gave me a full meal of a hamburger, fries, drink, and my cone – all free. He told my dad that he had to do something extra for someone with a perfect report card. To this my dad replied, "Well he got two B's so it's not perfect."

I spent a lot of my life trying to please him – or win. I became tenacious and competitive. Everyone is blessed in some way. My blessing was the ability to learn. Before I left elementary school, we had to complete IQ tests and I discovered a few years later that my parents were called in to school to discuss my education. The principal felt that it would be better for me to be placed in a private school after scoring high on the test. Unfortunately my parents could not afford to do this so I remained in public school and in high school excelled in all subjects graduating

14

salutatorian. My father was disappointed since I failed to graduate valedictorian. In my father's eyes, I should have worked harder. The fact that I was recruited by a college in Illinois during the summer of my junior year didn't sway his opinion. I actually could have gone to college a year early. The admissions office said I had completed all but one state requirement and I could do that in my first semester. It felt pretty good to be sought after by a college I must admit. However I'm glad I chose to complete my senior year in high school rather than go to college early. The next year I was awarded almost a full academic scholarship to Wabash College in Indiana where I obtained my Bachelor of Arts degrees in Biology and Chemistry. Although my father offered to pay for medical school, I knew he couldn't have afforded it. In fact, if it hadn't been for my scholarship, I couldn't have gone to college. He was a proud man that would never have admitted this, but the strain on my parents financially would have been severe.

My liberal arts education proved invaluable. I owe any success I've had in life to this. I read once, "Be so good they can't help but notice you." I believe in that and I daresay that all of my promotions were

15

a result. I was presented with opportunities that were never there for my dad or mom. The more I worked the more I realized that critical thinking, problem solving, and a strong work ethic were what dad referred to when he told me long ago about the importance of education. Of course there is only so much you can be taught in the classroom. The real work happens when you research those concepts outside the class. To this day, I'm still in love with learning – about anything. I read all the placards at historical sites and in museums. I read labels on almost everything to see if I know all the chemical stuff listed. But mostly I look up information all the time using Google. This tool is so great. I wish I had it during my high school and college years. I think it would have been easier.

I cannot emphasize this point enough. I have found that the phrase "knowledge is power" is absolutely true. There is a sense of pride when people come to you for help knowing that you're "smart" and can give them direction. On the other hand I never competed much in sports. As a child, I had health issues that prevented me from playing contact sports like my brother did. I was the nerd buried in books. I was active in the math club,

16

science club, media club, and Latin club. Consequently, I became adept at problem solving which paved the way to a decent career in business. Children often say that school is a waste of time because they'll never use what they're taught in school in the real world. I disagree. I may not be diagramming sentences today, but that exercise taught me invaluable communication skills. Some of the emails I read indicate that others seem to have been out that day in school.

I didn't start out well in school though. As soon as I entered kindergarten, I was sick a lot. My mom took me to the doctor when I was having a lot of trouble breathing and at times even turning blue. Our family doctor immediately sent me to the hospital where I spent about two weeks in an oxygen tent while tests were performed to find my problem. After a series of what can only be called barbaric scratch tests on my back, it was determined that I had asthma and was allergic to six main substances. These were milk, chocolate, ragweed, animal fur, dust, and cola. This meant that from the age of 5 until about the age of 18 (I eventually outgrew the allergies.) I could not have anything made with milk, chocolate, or cola. It

17

turned out that cat fur was my biggest problem respective to animal fur, but dogs were fine as long as I didn't have too much contact with them. This was good because my dad raised Beagles as hunting dogs. So now I was a small child unable to eat cheese, have a chocolate bar, or drink a coke. It was always interesting going to the ice cream shop after one of my brother's baseball games. Everyone had ice cream but I had an empty cone. I had to take large unappetizing chewable calcium tablets to replace the milk I couldn't have. My mom always looked for a milk substitute but in those days, the only thing available was soybean milk which was light brown in color and tasted awful. It was even gritty. YUCK! Eventually the science improved and there was white soybean milk available. I sometimes switched glasses with my brother at meals and would laugh hysterically when he took a sip and spit it out. My mom always got angry with me for that, but I think dad secretly thought it was a funny joke.

I was often sick and could not go to school so the teachers sent my work home with my brother. To keep up, I had to read a lot on my own and since I was restricted to rest, it worked out well. One of the problems with my asthma was that physical exertion would cause my lungs to constrict and I would have trouble breathing. Therefore, reading and homework were about the only activities I could do. We had monthly book orders in school so I could buy a lot of paperbacks to read. By the time I went to junior high, I daresay I had read more books than anyone in my class.

Reading all of these books created a foundation for analytical thinking, vocabulary, comprehension, spelling, deductive reasoning (detective books), geography (travel books), science, mathematics, and of course the literary skills of symbolism, metaphor, and foreshadowing. Not that you'll find any of that here but I recognize it when it exists.

For many years, I was angry with my father for pushing me so hard in school. I continually made the honor rolls having had great grades yet my father always seemed angry that I didn't receive A's 100% of the time. I realized later that he did that because he couldn't provide me a leg up anywhere. He wasn't friends with any business owners nor any executives in any companies. He knew that like him, the only way I could elevate

19

myself was to do it on my own. I would get no jobs in high positions as a result of any ties he had. As you can tell my father taught me a lot, but he had difficulty communicating and didn't know how to tell me the purpose of his methods. I would have to figure out the lessons myself. Fortunately for us both, I was eventually able to do so. I was left knowing that education is the foundation on which successes are built. I would pass on this knowledge to my own children, as well as many other young people if they wanted to listen. I also found that it doesn't matter if you don't go to an Ivy League school, but it certainly helps. Wabash College has long been considered the Ivy League of the Midwest. In my lifetime, I found that employers were impressed knowing I had degrees from Wabash. I had the credentials to go to Harvard or Princeton. Unfortunately, I couldn't afford the application fees, let alone the tuition and activity fees. My point is that I think a person should go to the best school they can afford. I also think a school should be picked based on mating the discipline they excel in teaching there to the discipline one wishes to pursue as a career.

Of course college isn't for everyone nor is it necessary for one to have a very fulfilling life. The most important thing is to find what you love to do and can spend hours and days doing it, because that's what a job is. It's working every day for many years to provide for a family and to make a living that's comfortable. If you can't find the endeavor that makes you happy and is exciting every day, you're doomed to going to a job you hate every day. Whatever it is you love doing, find a way to make that your source of income. If it takes training, get it. If it takes a degree, get that. But whatever you do, don't give up on doing what you like best, even if you have to get direction from others on what path to take. Another key is getting your education, training, or degree as early as you can. It's kind of like saving for retirement. The longer you wait, the harder it is to do.

21

CHAPTER THREE

Health

My father passed away when he was 72 years old. I'm convinced there were two major causes which could have been prevented in my opinion. One was the onset of diabetes that he ignored and the other was a lack of hobbies. The diabetes is what eventually caused his death. It led to blindness and eventually kidney failure. The diabetes began slowly. At first he was advised he could control it with diet. He didn't. That led to needing medication which combined with the proper diet could control his condition. He didn't do that either. This, of course, led to taking insulin shots. Dosages of these shots were steadily increased but without his help controlling diet, his condition continued to deteriorate. He lost his eyesight one morning and my mother and I took him to a specialist to see if there was anything that could be done to restore his sight. The doctor ran some tests with bright lights and asked a lot of questions as to dad's condition and how he had gotten to this point. When he left the room, my mother was saying that it seemed strange that this happened so suddenly. It was then that I became angry. "I'll tell you what happened! Every day for a few weeks or even months now, dad would wake up not being able to see. He'd sit up in his bed and after a few seconds, his sight would come back only he never told anyone he was having problems. God forbid he should actually listen to his doctor or get help! That would require admitting weakness!" Dad didn't say a word. He just sat in the chair quietly with his head slightly bowed. It was as if I had added humility and embarrassment to his feeling of weakness. When I saw that, I died inside. Dad was blind and I was being insensitive and taking what was left of his dignity. Once you say something emotionally damaging like that, it's done and you can't take it back. Since that day, I try to think before I speak. ...And I'm still working on it.

When the doctor had analyzed the tests, he came back suggesting a surgical procedure that might improve blood flow to the retina and thereby restore some of his eyesight. We agreed that it was worth trying even though he explained that it may not yield positive results. On the way home, I apologized to my dad and suggested that he do all

23

he could to follow any after care instructions to have the greatest chance of restoring his sight. Unfortunately the procedure did not help and dad remained blind. He became depressed but of course would never admit it. He hardly ever ventured out of his bed and mom put a CD player by his bed so he could listen to old TV shows recorded for the blind. My brother frequently went there to help take care of dad. He spent a lot of time with him and dad certainly appreciated it. Prior to that time, my brother didn't visit very often. I guess we really traded time with dad. Before he needed almost constant care, I was able to visit, help with home projects, mow his yard, or work on his cars. He and I even spent a lot of time driving hundreds of miles looking for a 1965 Impala. We must have looked at a dozen or more and even went to a KRUSE auction with the intent to bid on one. Instead, he found a 1950 Ford coupe and bought that. But then I changed jobs and was busy with my own kids so I didn't get to see dad as much. That was unfortunately when he started becoming ill and at that time, my brother who had been busy with his life, started spending more time with dad and I'm glad he became as close to him as I had.

I went through a stage of anger at my father for not listening to his doctor, but I eventually resolved to this: He lived as he wanted to live and he passed on his own terms. My terms are a bit different. I want to live as long as I comfortably can and enjoy as much time as possible with my family and friends. I therefore resolved to listen to my doctor when I reached the point in my life where my health required it. I suppose I could think of this as yet another lesson my father was teaching me. It was as if he had shown me what happens when you don't follow medical advice.

After the age of 30, I noticed that my intake of sugary sodas had started affecting my weight in a non-flattering way. I cut down on these substantially and eventually almost cut them out entirely, drinking only diet sodas and now water. I started getting annual physicals at the age of 46 hoping that if I ever developed any health issues, they would be detected early. At 55 some changes happened. My wife noticed that I seemed to have less energy and alcohol consumption seemed to affect me more. You haven't lived until you hear your wife tell your doctor, "He doesn't seem to be able to drink as much as he used to." The upshot was that I had a borderline low thyroid level and borderline cholesterol problems. I began daily low dose meds that corrected the problems. I have to say that had it not been for my wife, I would never have noticed that I had any problems to report to my doctor. This is why I take her to every appointment. She is more in tune with changes in my behavior than anyone and had she not spoken up, the thyroid test and others would not have been performed. I know I'm healthier because of it. As for my colonoscopy that same year, the doctor said he'd see me again at the age of 65.

I'm very healthy right now but there are multiple reasons for it. I think that having asthma my entire life gave me a lasting respect for good health and the desire to have it. In a way, having asthma made me appreciate my health even more after I had outgrown most of the allergen effects on my condition. My asthma now is triggered only by strenuous physical activity. I occasionally have problems in houses full of cats, but my own cat doesn't bother me. I mentioned earlier I was never involved heavily in contact sports so I've been free of joint and muscle problems. I've always worked with my head so physical labor never had the chance to deteriorate my body either. Anyway, back to dietary stuff. In addition to cutting down on sugar intake, I also stopped adding salt to my food around the age of 40 or so. I'm not salt free. I just don't add it to anything I eat. I drink in moderation and according to my phone, I walk about two and a half miles daily. I have a lot of friends who were involved in sports in their youth and they collectively have a lot of joint, back, and muscle problems. Other friends have physically demanding jobs in construction or factory work that has caused them the same type of musculoskeletal issues. This is why I feel fortunate to have had the opportunities I've had as a result of higher education. Mental work drains just as much energy as physical work but there is no drain on the body.

There are times when a person is ill. Most of these are colds and flu which also tax a person's immune system. I'm rarely sick and therefore have not compromised my immune system's ability to fight off minor infections. Long ago, I learned that my

27

grandmother was right to make hot toddies to fight viruses. In college I learned the structure of viruses and the difference between them and bacteria. It then became very apparent how alcohol fights viruses and why cold medicine has alcohol in it. Whenever I'm sick, I drink hot toddies, sleep with lots of blankets to break any fever and by the next morning I'm always much better. Most of the people I know that get sick with colds and flu are ill much longer than I ever am. Thanks Grandma. (Disclaimer – I'm not a doctor and am not providing medical advice. This is why I'm not providing my secret recipe for hot toddies.)

I completely intend to do all I can to stay healthy. For me that means getting an annual physical and making sure my wife goes with me to ask questions. If I develop any cancer or disease, I want to catch it as early as possible so an effective treatment can be had. I will also follow the doctor's instructions. If the treatment seems to not produce results, I'll return and get re-evaluated. The important thing is to follow instructions completely. Only then, can we discover what part of any treatment isn't working. I learned in my research studies that if you introduce more than one variable at a time, you can't determine which variable is impacting the solution.

I have also found that being active is very important to staying healthy. The adage "work hard, play hard" is very apropos. My philosophy has always been that life is short so do all you can to enjoy all it has to offer while you can. This is why I open myself to new experiences such as acting, singing, playing golf, or taking trips. I once met an 85 year old man who was very energetic. He exuded energy in his gait and conversation. He was a very lively, likeable fellow who struck me as a person who never met anyone he didn't like. I struck up a conversation with him and when he told me he was 85 years old, I was floored. His gray thinning hair and a few wrinkles indicated he was an older gentleman, but I had come to expect much less energy from people of that age. Others I had met of that age walked slowly and most times with the assistance of a cane or other means of support for failing balance. Their eyes are tired and weak and their speech is slow and full of effort. I asked him what his secret was to longevity. He simply said, "You have to kick the old man out. Don't let him in. Whenever the old man comes just kick him out!" And with that he started kicking the air with an exuberance that a martial arts instructor would be proud of. Although I laughed hard at his antics, I realized he was absolutely right. On those days that I start feeling old, I'll just "kick the old man out" and go sing karaoke, play golf, or maybe go on a cruise.

CHAPTER FOUR

Work

I started working when I was 15 by obtaining a work permit through school. My first job was in a dime store where I worked after school and on weekends as the stock boy. When summer came, I started working full days. After a couple of weeks, I was told that I was supposed to take a 10 minute break in the morning and another in the afternoon. This was in addition to my half hour lunch. I hated breaks. It wasn't enough time to read or do word puzzles like some of the other workers did although I did try. The problem with reading was that I spent a couple minutes trying to remember where I was in the story, another couple of minutes re-reading the last couple of pages to remind me what was happening, and then reading just a few pages before break would be over. In fact, whenever I got back to the book, I had to read the material I had read on my break anyway so what was the point? Usually during breaks I watched the clock, waiting to go back to work. I started using my breaks to make lists of what I had to do the rest of the day. At least by doing so I could be productive. Besides, I reasoned that during any given day, I had moments when I wasn't working. I was sure that all those times when I went to the restroom, or got a drink that they must have all added up to at least my break time if not more. My father once told me, "No one owes you a living." I was told when I got my first job to go to work early, do anything the boss asked, and stay late if needed. I was taught to always remember that I'm being paid and should be earning that pay for every minute I'm there. I think this is why I don't take breaks and work through my lunch to this day. Besides, as I mentioned earlier. Breaks are boring to me. I'm pretty sure I'm in a very small group of people with this perspective.

It was during my time in this store that the clothing store manager from a couple doors down, stopped me one day and asked if I would like to work for him on the days I didn't work at the dime store. At first I was concerned what my boss would think so I told him I had to check with her first. He told me then that he had already spoken to her about it and she would agree as long as I was OK with it. I readily agreed and soon was working almost full time at the age of 15.

The clothing store was different than the dime store. First of all, there wasn't much to stock, I mostly just rearranged the clothes that people had looked through and left a mess. The store manager had a list of daily tasks he wanted me to do and one of them was scraping any gum left by a patron off of the wood floors. I was doing just that one day when he rushed up to me and said, "What are you doing?" I thought I had done something wrong so I meekly replied, "Scraping the gum off the floor. It was on the list." He smiled and I was glad because I really thought he was mad at me. He said, "You're the first person I've ever had do that job without me asking." I found out the next week, I had been given a raise of $0.25 per hour. That was a lot in 1979.

Working more than one part time job emphasized a very valuable lesson. The more you work, the more you make. This must have been what dad was talking about to get ahead. With my summer earnings I was able to buy a very nice 35mm camera that year which was important later in my life when I used it professionally. Sometime during that summer, I also was recruited to work at the local Goodyear store as the janitor.

Periodically, I was also allowed to work on cars. It was a great learning experience for me. As you can see, I became a very hard worker immediately upon entering the workforce. To this day, I start working as soon as I arrive and don't stop until I leave. On many days I continue to work answering phone calls and emails after I've left for the day.

I define work ethic as how a person prioritizes their job compared to other things in their life. For example, I've had people call in sick when they have a hangover. I've had people call in to take the day off because the weather is nice. It's amazed me through the years what people have found to be more important than going to the place where they make the money that provides the living for their family. People have come to depend on me at my job and I'm proud of that. I will go to work when I don't feel well, but I also try to limit direct contact with anyone so as not to make them sick. Fortunately I don't become ill too often. I had some asthma trouble once and went to work. I couldn't walk very fast but I still did my job. For me, there is no point in giving anything less than 100% and that includes my job. I believe in giving my employer all that I am worth thereby making me worth all they give me. A person once told me that he always strived to save the company an amount equal to his annual salary. That way, he reasoned, there would not be a need to release him since he didn't cost them anything. I think that is a good way to think about it and you can't save the company money if you don't go to work. My father also told me, "Keep going to work every day. You do that and you'll be alright."

I also try not to complain too much about my job. I always remember that I went to them to get it. It was my choice. There have been a few times when I felt I had reached a plateau that I either needed to take on more responsibility or find another challenge. I was working as a production control manager for an automotive supplier, when I realized after 6 years I was no longer challenged. I discussed this with my plant manager but unfortunately there were no other positions available or new tasks to take. When I did find other employment, I gave them 4 weeks' notice. The very interesting thing about leaving was that I had a choice of jobs. Two different companies made me offers. In fact, they increased the offers once I was honest and told them I was considering another offer. This happened a second time in my career so this time I had learned my value. All of the education I spoke of earlier and the importance of critical thinking became something I was taking to the bank. Anyone can do this. Remember "Be so good they can't help but notice you"? Yeah. Do that.

At this point I have to say that although it may sound like I'm a workaholic, that isn't the case at all. I have a lot of fun and I enjoy life to the fullest. I am stressing the importance of being 100% focused on work when you're there. Remember, nothing else in life happens without the income you get from your job. And if that job isn't what you love doing, you're doomed to finding more ways to get out of it than doing it. That will negatively impact your family. Had I been a workaholic, maybe I'd have more wealth, but I wouldn't have all the life experiences I've had. And I've really enjoyed my off time. 100%.

I didn't easily find out what I was good at, however. I went to college wanting to go into medicine and perhaps be a pediatrician. After taking the MCAT and being accepted into medical

36

school, it was obvious that I couldn't afford it. Of course good 'ol dad said he'd pay for it, but he had no idea of the expense involved. In this one case of finances I made the right decision not to saddle us both with that debt. My second choice in a career was business. I liked the idea of someday running a company. I enjoyed being a leader in every organization I joined so this seemed to be a good fit. So when I graduated from college, I took a job with a Wall Street investment firm. I obtained the licenses to sell and approve the sale of mutual funds as well as life insurance. I did well there but after about five years, I discovered that some of my clients (and commissions) were being stolen from me by other representatives. Then when a manager suggested I perform a trade not in the best interest of my client, I had to leave. I couldn't work in an unscrupulous environment.

From there I went into manufacturing and I finally found what I was good at and what I loved doing. I started in the bottling industry as a microbiologist testing water samples to be sure they were pathogen free. I moved to production supervision, inventory control, environmental management, production control, and eventually to supply chain

37

management. It is here that I really found my niche. I analyze data constantly, determine best practices for lean manufacturing, and coordinate shipments to meet daily changing demands. I also became well versed in customer service over the years and am proud to say the companies I serve have a great deal of respect for me. They embarrass me with their praise. There is one solid and steadfast rule I won't break that has given me that praise. I won't lie to them. I have been chastised for giving them what I've been told was too much information, but I refuse to lie or cover up mistakes. I also under promise and over deliver which I preach to everyone I train. Never commit to something you can't execute. These foundations in my philosophy toward work have always paid me dividends.

You may be wondering at this point (as many people have – and asked me about it), why is a person with degrees in biology and chemistry working in logistics and supply chain management? Now I know I took a left turn from medicine and I'm pretty confident I would have really liked that field, but my education was not wasted. I mentioned in the education chapter that

I had learned well the skills of critical thinking and problem solving. To that can be added analysis and applicable research (gained from so much time in labs). These skills are immensely useful in my field. I daresay it's what has made me successful in my career.

CHAPTER FIVE

Hobbies

I got my driver's license at 16 which was also just after I started working. My father just so happened to need a new car for driving to work. (New is relative here. It was used; but new to him.) He told me that he couldn't buy me a car, but since I was working, I could use his car any time I needed it. For that privilege, I was to maintain the car. I think I only changed the oil in it and a couple of light bulbs. I was saving money from multiple part time jobs to buy my own car. Dad was looking for a good deal for me and by the time I was a senior I had a 1972 Chevy truck. Thus began my hobby of restoring antique vehicles. I loved that truck. It was two-tone orange and white with chrome side pipes, a cassette stereo with speakers in the doors, and cool wheels with white letter tires. I may have been a nerd, but I had a really cool truck. Anyway, one day it needed brakes and I took it to the station where dad got all his work done. Unfortunately I couldn't afford the cost, but the owner (a good friend of my dad's) suggested I do it myself. The pads were cheap and it was an easy job. Besides, I could learn about working on my truck. When I told my dad, he actually got excited. He said, "Sure, get the shoes and I'll help. I used to do all my own work on my '56 hardtop." At the time, I didn't fully grasp how important the words pads and shoes were going to be in my education. After obtaining the pads from the part store, dad told me to go ahead and take off the front wheel and to come get him when I had that done. The conversation when he came out went like this:

Me "I've got the truck on the jack and the wheel off."
Dad "Good let's see what it looks.......huh."
Me "What huh? Something wrong?"
Dad "Those are disc brakes."
Me "OK so they're disc brakes. Got it. What do we do first?"
Dad "I don't know. I've never worked on disc brakes before. You'll have to figure it out."

And with that, he went inside the house. I learned some very valuable information that day.

1. Pads are for disc brakes and shoes are for drum brakes.

41

2. It isn't necessary to remove the caliper by disconnecting the brake line to change the pads.
3. Bleeding air from the line is important – especially if you've removed the caliper spilled all the fluid on the porch.
4. I could learn a lot by taking things apart to figure out how they work.

The last item was the most important lesson. It taught me to never be afraid to try something new. Never be afraid to take something apart that doesn't work. If it doesn't work, I can't do any more damage to it no matter what I do. Since that day when my father unknowingly taught me the importance of confidence, I have completed both minor and major repairs on every vehicle I've ever owned. This includes everything from light bulbs to engine overhauls. I'm confident I have saved tens of thousands of dollars over the years and even made some extra money working on other people's vehicles. Thus my enamoration with classic vehicles deepened. Remember my first exposure was dad teaching me vehicle identification.

When I went to college, my dad asked if I could leave my truck at home for my brother to drive. My first thought was to tell him to work multiple jobs like I did to buy his own vehicle, but I knew that he was in sports and had to go to school really early for training so I left it home for him. To show his appreciation, he had it tuned up and in the process put hotter plugs in it to give it more power. I know he was trying to be nice and take care of the truck while he was using it, but the plugs burned a hole in a piston blowing the motor. Many years later, I bought another 1972 Chevy truck and it's currently in my garage. This time it was a Cheyenne Super which was the top of the line truck that year. This one is red and white. Red is my favorite color by the way. I still love that truck.

After I lost my truck I was in mourning for a while, but my dad promised to find me a great vehicle. He started looking for a 1962 Impala. This apparently was non-negotiable. It had to be a 1962. He searched for weeks in all the antique car sales magazines he could find. He eventually found one that was a good deal and took me to go look at it. I loved it. It needed some work but the

43

owner was going to finish a lot of it and in a week or so, we could pick it up. We made the deal and on the way home I had a conversation with my dad.

Me   "Hey Dad. Why were you so determined to get a 1962 Impala?"

Dad "What's wrong? Don't you think it's a good looking car?"

Me   "Oh yeah. It is. I was just wondering why it had to be a 1962."

Dad "You just said you liked the car. Don't you like the style the '62 has?"

Me   "Of course I do. I just don't understand why it had to be a '62. I mean, why not a '63 or '64? Or even a '56 like you had? What's so special about a '62?"

Dad "Oh for Pete's sake! What year were you born?'

Me   "'63."

Dad "Huh?"

Me   "I was born in 1963."

Dad "You were?"

Me   "Yes. In January."

Dad "Huh. Well you were DUE in '62"

And that's how I got a car built in the year I was almost born. I had that car a long time although it never did get fully restored. It wasn't really a restoration project at that time anyway. It was my family vehicle and many times, the only vehicle we had. During my life, I've had numerous older cars and trucks. They were cheap to buy and cheap to repair since I did all my own work. I was even able to customize some of them well enough for car shows where I won a few awards. I really liked going to car shows and met some really great people. I was able to learn a lot of skills from many of them and in turn passed along any knowledge I had acquired. I went to swap meets to find bargains on parts I needed for a project and sold any extra parts I didn't need. I went to auctions sometimes too and would buy items for the sole purpose of reselling for a profit. By doing this, the cost of trying to upgrade my vehicle was kept very low. The usual reality was after I'd get one problem fixed, another problem would immediately take its place. At least I always kept busy.

If I've learned anything from my father's passing, it's that hobbies are important. I was afraid that if

45

I had none, I was doomed to boredom and an early death. I wasn't sure that just an interest in cars would be enough to keep me occupied after retirement so I began playing golf. Then I got involved in Community Theater. I started to travel which sometimes included taking vacation trips on a motorcycle (extension of the car hobby). You see my father had only one hobby. He liked antiques so he would go to auctions and buy items he thought were more valuable than what he paid. He used to say he was going to open an antique store upon retirement but he never did. From my perspective, it's important to have varied interests so that if one activity becomes boring, you have another to keep you busy. So ... I have more than one hobby.

I don't know what my handicap is at golf. In fact, it's too much work to find out what my handicap would be given that it's probably embarrassingly high anyway. Believe it or not, the way to calculate handicap involves playing certain courses that qualify in the calculation and something called the course slope has to be used to do so. There are also a specific number of rounds that need played. For this reason, if anyone invites me to play golf and they have a handicap, I already know I'm not qualified to play. I play golf for fun and to relax. I have a lot of friends that feel the same way. Whenever we can, we get together to play a scramble round. Since we're just out to have fun, playing the best ball is faster and ultimately more enjoyable. This is definitely a hobby I can retire to.

At about the time my daughter was 12 years old, I got a Harley. It was a 1970 Electraglide and was a really nice bike. In fact, I took it to motorcycle shows and won some awards with it. That old shovelhead sounded fantastic. It had a wonderful signature lope in the rumble when it idled. My son really became interested in riding and at 15 obtained his permit. The cool thing about having a motorcycle permit at 15 is that you can't take passengers. On one particular day, he rode the Harley to school and when he came outside, there was a group of kids all around the bike admiring it. He joined them pointing out really cool items on it such as the custom engraving, the fish tail pipes and so on. He then threw his leg over the saddle to the astonishment of the crowd, started it up, and rode off.

47

It was sometime later when I bought my Indian Motorcycle. A beautiful 2002 black and silver Roadmaster with saddlebags and a windshield. The windshield came off quickly as I enjoyed having my face in the wind. I still had the Harley so I gave it to my son. I really enjoyed riding my motorcycle. In fact, I loved it so much that I wrote a column for Abate of Indiana's magazine, The Hoosier Motorcyclist for two years. The column was called, "The MacGyver Factor". I'll get to the meaning of that later. I wrote about motorcycle safety and maintenance. Riding trips were another subject always fun to discuss. It allowed me to introduce people to places worth riding to and having fun. The most memorable trip I took was with my son to the Great Smokey Mountains. We gassed up our bikes and at the first stoplight, I asked him which way he wanted to turn. He asked, "Which is which?" I said, "If we turn right, we'll go north and ride around the Michigan loop and see the great lakes. If we turn left, we'll ride south and take the Dragon's Tail in the Smokies." He chose left. As we were riding the first few days, he didn't want to ride beside me. He was 17 and had limited road experience on the Harley. By the time we were coming home, we were riding side by side and I looked over to see him on the inside of a curve with his right hand on the throttle and his left hand holding a lollipop in his mouth. There was a point on our trip when we were coming through the mountains (and stopped just outside Gatlinburg for a break) when a car that had been following us stopped with us. The driver got out and rushed up to us asking if we were professional riders. We laughed as we replied no and asked why he thought so. He said he'd been following us down the mountain road and swore that we could have put a broom handle between us and it would never have moved. He said he'd only seen that kind of precision riding in shows. My son beamed. Another day later when we rode the Dragon's Tail, he was so good that he stayed right behind me and my Indian even though his floor boards and exhaust mounts scraped the road on a lot of the curves. (His Harley had a lot less ground clearance.) I'll never forget that trip and how my son became a true motorcyclist.

It wasn't long after that trip that we found ourselves visiting friends in Chicago as part of an Indian Motorcycle riding group we belonged to. On

49

that weekend we were riding north of Chicago in Wisconsin on our way to meet some more friends. When we were about five miles from our objective, I noticed that my son was falling behind and eventually stopped. I turned around to help and found that his shifter had broken. We limped the bike back to a convenience store / gas station and I called my friends to let them know of our problem. I then had an idea. I went inside and bought a pair of jumper cables. I took the shifter off the bike with the thought of welding it together with the cables. I knew the battery on the bike would be too weak for this so I asked a guy parked next to us in a pickup truck if I could use his. He readily agreed saying, "I've got to see this." I then took a penny out of my pocket and clamped it to the positive lead grounding the shifter with the other. I had almost completed the weld when our friends rode up. One of them asked, "What the hell are you doing?" When I told them I was welding his shifter together so we could get back to Chicago, they called me "MacGyver". The funniest part of this is that about a year later a lot of us gathered in Ohio for the weekend at another friend's house. Some had been with us in Chicago and some

50

hadn't. We were all sitting at the table and dinner conversation was about road stories. Suddenly one of our friends from Wisconsin got very excited.

"Guys, Guys! You have to hear this. There was this dude stuck on the road and he WELDED his bike together with a pair of jumper cables and a penny!"

Everyone at the table, including me, started laughing.

"No really! It's true! A friend of mine from Milwaukee told me about it and he never says stuff like that if it isn't true!"

We were all laughing and then our host said, "We know it's true. He's sitting right there. THAT's MacGyver." And that's how I received my biker nickname. All bikers have nicknames. A friend of mine once rode through some fresh white paint spilled on the road and we called him Chalky. Another friend once failed to put his kickstand down and his bike fell over when he parked it. He became "Kickstand". The real fun was going to a bar in a group where the bartender wanted to know our names. Being polite people we obliged. "This is Snake, Birdman, Chalky, and MacGyver.

51

I'm Doc." Incidentally, Birdman was my son's nickname. He has had more than one bird hit him while riding so we started calling him Birdman. Bikers aren't known for being kind with nicknames.

As for theater, I got involved later in my life. I began performing on stage regularly at the age of 31. The only experience I had prior to that was a one-time stint in high school. You see when I was a senior in high school I was in a production of "Bye Bye Birdie". I had not yet been in a theatrical performance and true to my philosophy of trying anything once, I auditioned for the show. If you know the show, there are a lot of high school age characters which is why it's performed in a lot of high schools. All of the high school boys were played by our group of what can only be called jocks. They had the perfect looks. Athletic, good looking, and many were tall. Unfortunately they couldn't sing. Something I've always found useful in a musical. I was cast as the Mayor of the city. I wasn't tall or athletic, but I could sing. So the director positioned me behind the curtain with a mic to sing all the male parts in the opening of the show. At this point I need to interject that for all of my junior high and high school career, I was in band. I played trumpet and since choir classes were always held the same time as band, you were in one or the other, but not both. It was in band that of course I learned to read music which was also very helpful for performing in a musical. Even without the formal voice training, I somehow managed to figure out how to sing. I credit my mother with this ability. She has a wonderful singing voice and I'm sure I inherited her musical genes. It wasn't until my second marriage however that I learned to sing properly from my wife.

Twelve years after high school, I was given tickets to see "Little Shop of Horrors" at our local community theater. I loved the show and poured over the program to see who these fabulous actors and singers were. On the back page I noticed that in a few days auditions were being held for "Seven Brides for Seven Brothers". I had to go. I mean, I had seen the movie and I really like it. I figured it would be really fun to be a part of a live show.

When I went to the audition I found I was not prepared. There were people that had brought

53

their own sheet music to sing to and were rehearsing dance moves getting ready for their turn. I had nothing. No music nor any idea what they wanted to hear me sing, and as for dancing? I forgot that there was a lot of that in the movie. Through some miracle I was cast in the show as one of the suitors in town, and as a very good friend of mine said, "The rest is history." I've been fortunate enough to play many leading roles in stage productions in many theaters. I was also honored with a best actor award for my performance as Felix Unger in "The Odd Couple". I have even performed with the Indianapolis Opera but that's another story. I really love being on stage especially with my wife. She sometimes will be in productions without me but this is because it's her job. She works as a professional in music videos, commercials, print advertisement, and of course stage performances. For me, theater is a hobby. I love performing but it truly is a lot of work. A typical show requires three to four rehearsals per week for about 6 weeks resulting in 4 to 6 performances. For this reason, I really don't want to be in a performance if my wife is not there with me. I have thought about working full time as an actor once I retire, but my wife told me that wouldn't work. She said that I'd be really good at it and get lots more offers than her which would make her jealous and angry. Of course she was kidding but can you see the support I have from her? The truth is that male performers are harder to find. That significantly lowers the standard. She says that I'm really talented, but I know where the real talent is between us. I just have less competition. It reminds me of grade school actually. I got to play kickball because everyone played. And I was always picked close to last.

The point of all this is that I found activities of interest so that I would always have a zeal for life and what it has to offer. I'll never be bored after my career is over. There is so much to see and so much to do beyond sitting on a sofa watching others live life on television. I can't imagine having nothing to do each day. However I also don't discount the comfort of doing nothing. But if I ever feel that old man creeping in, I'll be sure to kick him out.

CHAPTER SIX

Stress

I started writing a manuscript years ago on the non-existence of stress. After a while, I realized that there wasn't enough content on the subject to warrant an entire book. Oh I could have droned on about beliefs and theories but it's such a non-specific condition as defined that I shelved the idea. However, my philosophy has not changed. Stress only exists if I create it and therefore since I choose not to create it, I have none. Don't get me wrong. I understand the physical existence of stress in mechanical objects such as tension on a spring, or the resistance created when a metal rod is bent or stretched. In these cases stress increases until either the spring or the metal rod breaks. The first use of the term stress to describe a human condition is credited with Dr. Hans Selye in the 1920's. Thus began a very lucrative market in stress treatment. The basis for Dr. Selye's identification was that all patients in hospitals shared something in common no matter what their ailment. He noticed that no matter what the reason for their hospitalization, they all looked similar with pallor, drooping eyes, and generally...well....sick. This was indeed a breakthrough. It established that there could be some common symptom or cause for every illness. If it could be determined what that was, a treatment might be established to cure illnesses more easily. Dr. Selye suggested that this commonality must be some physical stress causing sickness. I realize this seems a bit obvious and even perhaps a little contrived but in his final analysis, we find the groundwork for a huge industry. He believed that stress is a non-specific strain on the body which causes the release of non-specific stress hormones. How about that for a conclusion? Basically it boiled down to this. People that look sick must have something wrong with them, but since we can't identify the common cause or provide a list of symptoms, we'll just say it's non-specific. Since it is non-specific, we are open to any number of gadgets, exercises, vitamins, tonics, or snake oil you can think of for purchase as a cure. And I've seen some doosies, all touting the purpose of "relieving stress". Today almost every ailment is considered to be caused by "stress". And anything that makes you feel

57

nauseous, tired, listless, or otherwise not yourself can be attributed to "stress". Now I know I'm oversimplifying this, but we have reached a point where as a society we tend to overcomplicate things and it drives me up the wall. (One of my father's better sayings.) I suppose that makes me stressed. I will concede that when faced with obstacles beyond my control, something inside of me causes my heart to race and my breathing to become more rapid. To me this is nothing more than the "fight or flight" mechanism which has now become included as the first stage in Dr. Selye's theories on stress. Biologically, there are indeed hormones triggered when I am faced with danger, but how this became equivocated with life pressure is a wonder to me.

I agree that sometimes there are pressures at work to meet deadlines or to solve problems, but I can only control what is within my ability. For example, I cannot receive parts that are not shipped. I CAN request a supplier to ship earlier and I CAN schedule expedited freight. I can even pick up the parts myself if the supplier has them made. However, there is no reason to worry about their arrival once I have done all I can. Constant questions of when will they arrive, how long will it take to unload the truck, or "tell me again when we can have them for production" are not going to make me anxious. Why should it? Why worry about traffic, weather, fallen trees, blown motors, or any other malady that would affect the delivery? I have no control over any of those conditions and therefore choose not to concern myself with them.

I hear people say they are "stressed out". I have no idea what that means but I choose to define it this way. 'I have chosen to concern myself with so many things that I can do nothing about, that I am incapable of concerning myself with my job, responsibility at home, playing with the kids, making dinner, fixing the dryer, changing the oil, or (insert controllable task here). The problem is that if I allowed myself to submit to so-called stress that I would get nothing accomplished. Eventually that would lead to being depressed because nothing was getting done. That leads to family problems, work problems, income problems and any manner of other issues. This is why I refuse to believe in the existence of stress as an actual condition.

59

I also hear a lot of people say, "I can't handle the stress." What stress? You mean the mental condition you created when you got lost in your own personal concerns about stuff you could do nothing about? Like you suddenly are incapable of doing your job because someone put items you work with in a different spot? I see no reason for people to get upset because the candy machine has been removed. I actually had a person walk off the job because their workbench had been moved and they couldn't handle "the stress". They never came back.

Here's what I know. There are things in life I can't control yet bother me. The key is to understand that I can't control it so there is no reason to worry. I don't like cold weather but I have chosen to live in an area that has a few cold months each year. I made the choice. I accept the cold. I think there are things we can improve at work but if my ideas don't get implemented, I accept it. I accept the fact that it wasn't implemented. I don't stop trying to get it done. But I also don't worry about how long it will take or if it ever will.

I also hear a lot of people saying they're "stressed out" about unknown situations like what to have for dinner. I just don't get it. Why be concerned about having to make a decision? Whatever I decide, there will be consequences. Some may be good or some may be bad but no matter what, they will exist and I may have to then make another decision. I might have to go out to eat. I have a lot of theater friends that seem to worry whether or not they will get a part. I don't understand that either. Once the audition is over, my part is done. There is no point in worrying about it so I don't. I'll be happy if I get the part and if it's a role I want badly, I'll probably be upset if I don't get the part. But two things are clear. The audition is mine - the casting decision is not.

I've shared my thoughts on so-called stress with a lot of people and I get a lot of responses like "it's not that easy" or "you don't have my stress". First of all it is ABSOLUTELY that easy. It's easy to not concern yourself with things you have no control over because there's nothing you can do to change them. Moreover, since you're the one that created the concern, you can just as easily forget it. And no I don't have your stress. In fact, I don't have mine because I didn't make any to have. Maybe if you would quit creating things to think about that you can't affect, you wouldn't have any either. Bottom line is either you control situations or situations control you. And if situations control you, that could lead to medication.

CHAPTER SEVEN

Relationships

Being a nerd was never conducive to an active love life. I was never what you'd call a looker in high school. I weighed 98lbs at high school graduation at a height of 5' 8". I'm happy to say that I have maintained my height. I was always small and didn't have much of a physique since physical activity was limited to feeding and watering our dogs. I tried playing baseball and basketball as a child but would have trouble breathing very quickly. I therefore abandoned becoming a professional in any sport and concentrated on my studies. Interestingly I was asked to join the swim team as a diver when I was in Junior High. (We didn't have Middle School in 1975.) I had been doing very well in the gymnastics portion of physical education and the coach thought that ability would make me an excellent diver. Although he explained to my mother that it was less physically demanding than swimming, she was concerned for my health and I did not join the team. In fact, I never learned how to do more than a backflip. But once I got to college, I began working out with weights and even competed in powerlifting competitions. I lifted in the 132 lb weight class. My best performance was a deadlift of 365 lbs, a squat of 280 lbs and a bench press of 200 lbs. I had expanded to the proper size for my height. When I attended my fifth high school reunion, the girls noticed.

I met my first wife my senior year in high school and was married just before my junior year in college. Our relationship was a young love that resulted in two wonderful children. Both are happy and doing well and I'm very proud of them. I met my second wife on stage. She was a children's librarian yet had been a stage performer for years. She had professional experience in musical theater and in the opera. I was impressed and told her that I too would like to sing in the opera. It could be really fun. She just laughed and said maybe I could someday. Some months later, she called me at work to tell me that the director of the Indianapolis Opera Chorus had asked her to sing in a cantata at his church. I asked her to see if he could use a baritone. He could. After the cantata was over we were both asked to perform in the upcoming, "Opera Goes to the Movies" performance at Clowes Hall in Indianapolis. After that, she helped me get involved in other opera performances in Indianapolis, and later when we moved to the St. Louis area we were both able to sing with the St. Louis opera. Had it not been for her help in training my voice, I would never have had these opportunities to sing with opera companies.

My wife and I have a wonderful relationship. After moving to southern Illinois, I decided that if we cut back on expenses, we could live on my salary and she could pursue her dream of being a full time actress. This afforded us the opportunity to define our relationship roles more traditionally. She would do the cooking, cleaning, and laundry while I would take care of the yard, vehicle maintenance, and general repairs. She likes to call herself a submissive housewife. I like to call her my helpmeet. Major expenses such as home remodeling, new vehicles, vacations, or relocation are my decisions as head of the household. This does not mean that I don't seek out and listen to my wife's advice. It simply means that I am the one making the final decisions on these matters as they are directly related to the provision for my

65

family. Once a decision has been made, the discussion is ended. This is a very important part of our happiness. To illustrate my point, I have an anecdote. My wife had a minor accident in her car that resulted in a discussion of repairing the car or buying another. I decided to give her the car I had been driving to work which was in much better shape than the one involved in the accident and buy a different one for me. This is also something I feel strongly about. My wife should always have the newest car with the lowest miles. If there is anything remotely possible to go wrong on the road, I want it to be with me. I also don't want her to be worried about her car's reliability so of course I keep it well-maintained. But I digress. I was going to buy a different car for me. I wanted certain features in my car. I wanted a two seater convertible that achieved at least 25 miles per gallon. Since it was only the two of us and we already had a larger sedan, I saw no need to have a sedan or an SUV as a second car. Now my wife had very clear opinions on this. First, she doesn't like convertibles. The wind bothers her ears. Second, she thinks they're unsafe because if they roll over, there is no top for protection. Therefore,

I found and purchased a used hard top convertible with roll bars behind the seats. She doesn't like driving or riding in the car but she never questions my decision to buy it.

I will say this. In order for a relationship like ours to work, the head of the house has to recognize their responsibility. It's not just the wife. Yes, she has dinner on the table nightly when I come home from work greeting me daily dressed as if she would be going out. I always have clean clothes to wear neatly folded and put away in my bureau or hanging in my closet, and the house is always neat and tidy. But I have to give her something to be worthy of this. I make sure that regular maintenance is performed on our cars or repairs are made if needed. I maintain the lawn and take out the trash and recycling. I provide the necessary income to pay the monthly bills with enough left over for sundries. She likes to get her hair and nails done to which I never say no. I try to fulfil any special requests quickly such as cleaning toilets (she hates that job), or unclogging drains. If an appliance has an issue, it is my responsibility to either fix it or replace it. Yes, we have a wonderful relationship and it's because we

67

have defined and agreed upon each other's roles. The most important part of our bond is deciding that there should be one person as the head of the house. This is crucial in that it provides the platform for trust. I trust in her counseling and she trusts in my leadership to make good decisions. There are entire books written on this subject and I daresay, she's read every one of them.

My father and mother had a similar relationship so I guess it's no wonder that I would follow their lead. My dad always taught me to respect women. The usual behaviors were both taught and exemplified such as opening doors, walking on the street side of the sidewalk when escorting a lady, standing at a table until the lady is seated, or carrying packages. On these things, my belief is simple. Since I respect women, I should show that respect with kindness and courtesy. I therefore do things for my wife so that she does not need to. I find it ridiculous that some women would find my actions offensive. My wife chooses to clean and cook for me out of respect for me and I don't find that offensive at all so why should any woman find it offensive that I mow the lawn?

I love my wife. This is why I am driven to make her happy. Nothing makes me feel so good as to see her beaming with happiness. Every morning before I leave for work, I fix the covers on the bed I recently vacated and go to her side. As I lean down slowly and gently come close to her face, I can feel the softness of her cheek against mine, the warmth emanating from under the covers around her neck and onto my face as she turns to meet me. Then I see it. That slight upturn of the corners of her lips causing her checks to flush. "There's my smile." I whisper to her. I kiss her softly, tell her I love her and to get some rest. Then I watch as she snuggles back under the covers – still smiling.

CHAPTER EIGHT

Finances

When I was young I made a lot of bad decisions. I married while I was still in college and apparently then as now, that simple act puts you on the list of every company that will try to sell you everything from vacuum cleaners to dishware on convenient easy to make payment plans. In addition, every retail store, fuel station, and credit card company will offer you cards that are so easy to use for any purchase imaginable. I did not manage these offers well, but I have seen many people fair even worse than I. It always sounds great. You can have new items immediately and pay for them over time. The issue for me was that I failed to realize that over the course of the payment plans, I would have paid for that item many times over before I was done. This prevented me from saving money for emergencies which of course resulted in using a credit card for them. More payments. It was a vicious cycle that literally took years to erase. I learned too late that you can't live beyond your means no matter how hard you try. I see these television shows where people are buying houses.

Young people in their 20's with small children buying a larger home so each child can have their own room. I always wonder what these people do for a living because their budgets are always over 250K and a large amount of the show participants are spending over 400K. I cringe thinking of how they're ever going to get out of debt and retire.

My father always told me to save some of the money I earned every time I was paid. It wasn't that I didn't listen. I just couldn't figure out how to do it. Every dime I made was needed for bills. It never occurred to me that I was responsible for creating my own bills. Dad was right when he told me to work hard and either get a good education or work overtime. What I missed was the lesson on only spending 90% of what you make. I never had a problem knowing what I could afford with respect to a place to live or vehicles. My problem was failure to see how all the small ticket items added up creating problems with paying the electric bill or the gas bill. And to top it all off, I blamed everyone else but me. How dare they sell me a vacuum cleaner for $10 per month. I told them my income, couldn't they see that I was unable to afford that? I mean with the

71

kitchenware at $15, the gas card at $25, the sofa at $15, and the credit card at $20? Yes I was stupid. And you can't fix stupid. You can only stop the disease by finally paying them off and don't repeat the process. Unfortunately for me, that meant a visit to the court to make payment arrangements. Of course that created problems too. For many years I had that black cloud hanging over my head and when I really needed credit, I had to pay higher interest. There's that vicious cycle again. I couldn't afford to buy the things I did so I had to borrow more money to pay off the debt creating even more debt. Oh and as an added bonus I would stay in debt for a long time because since by now it was obvious to everyone I didn't have good payment history, my interest rate would be higher. I found it truly reprehensible that I had gotten into debt when I couldn't afford to be yet when my income went up, so did my debt. It seemed like every time I made more money, the cost of using it went up at the same rate thereby guaranteeing that I would never have any disposable income to save. It was as if the business world had decided that I was to be held down and not allowed to succeed by way of higher interest rates. I realized that unless I made some significant changes, I would never enjoy a nice home, a nice car, or a comfortable retirement.

The solution was easy and something that had I implemented in my 20's, I might be a wealthy man today. Here's the secret. I had to spend much less than I made. There's a shocker. And by that I mean no financing of any item costing less than $5000. It still took a while but along the way a funny thing happened. Those items like new bedroom furniture, a new washing machine, or a new television were never missed. I simply said no to financing. If I really needed something, I saved enough cash to buy it. Eventually, I cleared my debt and was even able to save some money finally. I'm still behind where I should be for a comfortable retirement but at least I have a plan and hopefully, I'll be able to make it.

CHAPTER NINE

Vices

I have two vices. I think that is plenty for one person to have. I haven't always had these vices. I was 12 years old practicing gymnastics on our front yard on a Saturday when my dad came home from work. He came to me and asked me if I wanted the rest of his beer. My uncle had dropped him off and in those days the passenger could drink and there was no open container law. That 6oz of beer was my first drink. I didn't have another until I was 20 and in college. For the next 20 years or so, I drank very little. I would estimate consuming a single case of beer during all those years combined.

Once my children were grown, however, I began drinking socially. I have learned a lot over the years about alcohol. For example, I have learned that preferences change with alcohol just like they do with food. As a child for example, I hated broccoli and squash. As an adult, I find this a fantastic side dish to a well-prepared steak. My taste for beer progressed from the light variety to the darker more stout products. I found that Irish whisky backed with a stout Irish beer was very tasty. I tried to like tequila and one New Year's Eve, my brother-in-law and I drank a few with lemon and salt. I don't think I've had tequila since.

The same taste progression is true for liquor. Irish whisky was good and I wanted to try other varieties of whiskey. (Whisky is from Ireland and whiskey is from the United States.) Now understand that all of my discussion of this vice pertains to taste and flavor. I never have nor will I ever drink with the goal of getting drunk. I have been inebriated to the point of getting sick and I hated it. Anyway I digress. We were talking about whiskey. I never liked the cheap whiskey. I find it too harsh and only good for those people yelling, "shot, shot, shot" at the bar which I have always found silly. Kentucky distilleries produced much smoother products to my taste and most is of course bourbon. I learned a lot about bourbon and progressed to many good varieties. I have even had the pleasure of tasting both the 10yr and 15yr varieties of Pappy Van Winkle. My list of favorites is now very long but at least it's easy to buy me a gift.

Somewhere in the middle of my whiskey / bourbon journey I tried scotch. Scotch is a much more complex whiskey requiring much more time to age due to the nature of the barrels it's aged in. I could never acquire a taste for the cheaper scotches. They taste like cheap whiskey to me. I think blended scotches should be used for blending. Good examples of great cocktails for blended Scotch would be a Rob Roy or a Godfather. There are many varieties of scotch and there are so many good ones. I have learned that I don't like the ones that have a strong peat flavor so scotch produced in the Islay region tastes like kerosene to me. However, like bourbon, I have a long list of brands I find pleasing especially from the Highland and Speyside regions.

On to vice number two. I smoke cigars. I prefer to practice my two vices together but often I cannot. There are a large number of laws across this nation preventing the pairing of these vices. Drinking establishments that allow smoking of any kind will soon be extinct. I went to a bar once years ago that allowed cigarette and pipe smoking but not cigars. I cut part of my cigar, put it in my pipe and smoked it. Take that, authority. I had a pipe as the result of a story relayed to me by a bar patron a few years earlier than the no cigars but pipes are OK incident. I was smoking outside of a bar when a person came up to me and said, "I see you smoke cigars. Where's your pipe?" I told him I only smoked cigars and hadn't tried a pipe. He went on to explain that every cigar smoker he knew always carried a pipe and smoked the last of their cigar in it. This made absolute sense to me. I had been smoking my cigars down as far as I could without setting my fingers or nails on fire. I got quite good at it too. I could smoke a cigar down to almost nothing to hold, but the idea of never having to keep changing the fingers I was using to hold the cigar was genius to me. Now not all cigar smokers are as cheap as I am. Some even leave an inch or more and throw it out. My reasoning is simple. If I pay $10.00 for a cigar (which is about the average cost of good ones that are hand rolled) and the cigar is six inches long, that's $1.67 per inch. I don't want to throw away $1.67 every time I smoke. That adds up. Etiquette prevents just grabbing nubs out of ashtrays so as you read this, don't do that. Just don't.

77

Cigars are also a journey like good liquor. Many years ago while working in the digital graphic design industry, my boss gave me a cigar to celebrate the successful closing of a business deal. That led to another celebratory cigar, gifts from me to my boss of cigars, and so on. Thus began the start of my preferred method of relaxation. I also became quite adept at pairing cigars with the proper brandy, cognac, bourbon, or scotch. Of course this required a lot of research and research is a strength of mine having performed so much of it in college. I experimented with many different brands and types of cigars to find which ones I liked. Along the way I also experimented with different alcohol combinations with those cigars. In my travels both for business and for pleasure, I visited a lot of different lounges that sold cigars to sit down, relax, and enjoy a smoke. Most of them had lockers you could rent to store your cigars. This allowed them to be kept at the proper humidity for the best condition. Although at times I was a frequent visitor to some shops, I never had the desire to rent a locker. I saw no advantage and indeed many times, it was almost a zen experience with no one there but me and my one, hour long to smoke, cigar. You must know by now that I am an energetic sort that doesn't like to sit still for long so while cigar smoking affords me relaxation, sitting alone while enjoying the cigar was too much. I at least needed conversation.

And that leads us to the shop I currently patronize. I now have a membership at my local cigar shop and regularly visit with my friends who are also members. Just like all hobbies, there are a lot of items that can make the experience more enjoyable and this vice is no different. I have an array of cutters, torch lighters, humidors, and pipes for any type cigar. I also have cigar related décor such as wooden wall hangings that look like cigars. (Another offshoot of the hobby as I made these myself. I also gave some to friends as gifts.) I really like this shop and glad I've become a member. We have had a wide and varied range of conversations on any topic imaginable. We have often said that many of the world's problems could be solved simply with people sitting down together and discussing them over a fine cigar.

CHAPTER TEN

Wrapping it up

I said in the beginning that I've had what I consider to be a pretty good life. And I owe this life to my parents and the educational opportunities I had more than anything else. Of course I also feel that I've made more good decisions than bad. I have had the good fortune to be proud of many things in my life and have had at least what I feel are many accomplishments. Some of these weren't germane to the subjects covered here and so were omitted from the discourse. Suffice it to say, I don't have to reminisce about "glory days". I'm still living in them.

Here are the hot points that summarize what I have learned in my life which I have shared with others when asked for advice.

- I have always tried to remain positive, to look at the bright side. It has given me not only hope but happiness.
- I believe in the value of a good education. I am still learning and will do so as long as I live. Being educated has provided me with a

80

good income which in turn helped me provide for my family.

- I think it's extremely important to get annual physicals and follow the doctor's orders. Ask questions, do research, find answers, and stay healthy.
- I think the key to vocational happiness is finding what you're good at and what you love to do. If you're lucky, they're the same thing. I always want to earn what I make so I'll be worthy of making what I earn.
- Having hobbies is important to me for health, happiness, and overall well-being. Keeping my mind busy has always been important to me.
- Stress only exists in me if I create it. There is no advantage to creating stress so I don't do it and as a result, I have none.
- I found that being happy in a relationship means defining roles and agreeing to those roles. That simple act in my marriage created trust and respect for us both.
- Finances are difficult to deal with and I wish I had not established a debt base so young. I finally figured out NOT to finance anything

that cost less than $5000, but it sure cost me more than that to learn it.

- I have my vices but the key is moderation. Too much of anything is bad for you. Besides, good scotch, good bourbon, and good cigars are meant to be savored. Therefore I take my time to enjoy them.

Someday I will retire and on that day, I will be happy knowing that I have another chapter to begin in my life and plenty to keep me busy. And being busy is the best way I know to kick the old man out.

Made in the USA
Columbia, SC
29 December 2024

50814727R00046